SURVIVING LIFE IN THE FAST LANE

A DISCUSSION GUIDE BY TIM KIMMEL

Based on the book *Little House on the Freeway*

NAVPRESS ◭ ®

A MINISTRY OF THE NAVIGATORS
P.O. BOX 6000, COLORADO SPRINGS, COLORADO 80934

The Navigators is an international Christian
organization. Jesus Christ gave His followers the
Great Commission to go and make disciples
(Matthew 28:19). The aim of The Navigators is
to help fulfill that commission by multiplying
laborers for Christ in every nation.

NavPress is the publishing ministry of The
Navigators. NavPress publications are tools to
help Christians grow. Although publications
alone cannot make disciples or change lives,
they can help believers learn biblical discipleship, and apply what they learn to their lives
and ministries.

Contents

Introduction

Life carries us along at a furious pace. Amidst the hurry and haste we instinctively realize our need for rest—peace in the midst of the storm. Jesus Christ offers us this rest for the weary. In this study we will explore the keys to genuine rest.

We all have busy schedules. For this reason this study is designed so that you don't need to prepare in advance. It includes a section that encourages you to apply the truths of each session during the following week. Scripture references are written out for your convenience. You will want to have a copy of the study guide in which to write your thoughts and responses during the discussions.

Each session contains the following sections:

Warm-up. The first question in this section usually requires the sharing of insights gained during the week from the previous week's session. The second question is designed to get you thinking about the topic to be discussed in this session.

Text. This material is adapted from the book *Little House on the Freeway*. If you want a more in-depth look at the topics discussed you will enjoy reading *Little House on the Freeway*. Reading the book, however, is not necessary for successfully completing this study. You can decide as a group if you want to read the text before or during the session.

Questions. These questions will help you take a look at how Scripture deals with the issues raised in the text.

You will also be challenged to apply these truths to practical life experiences. You don't have to look at these questions before the group time, although doing so will add to what you will be able to contribute to the discussion. There are arrows (▶) beside some questions. This denotes optional questions. The leader may choose to skip these questions if time is limited.

Into Our Lives. This section has further applications of the truths discussed in the session. You should do one of these activities each week. This will not require a lot of time, but will add to the impact of the session on your life. Insights from this section will be shared at the beginning of the following session.

For Meditation. This section contains quotes to stimulate further thought on the topic of the session. These quotes can be used during the discussion or for reflection later.

In Search of Peace and Rest

WARM-UP
- Give your name (only if group members don't already know each other).
- Think back to a typical day during the past week, and briefly describe how you spent your time, giving the group a sketch of what your day was like.

THE HURRIED HOME

❚❚ Whatever happened to uncluttered and uncompli- cated lives?

Maybe every generation asks the same question. But not every generation has had to deal with pressures like ours has. We're teetering on the edge of the twenty-first century knowing that we must plunge into the future but not sure we're ready.

It seems like only yesterday we were plowing the lower forty, walking to school, going to town once a week, and getting to bed by eight o'clock. Millions of people who made their debut on our planet in the early part of this century remember when their town looked like the set of "Little House on the Prairie."

But Walnut Grove has changed a lot since they added the Pizza Hut, the Seven-Eleven, and the unisex hair salon. Quiet, simple lives have given way to off ramps, automatic teller machines, and Quarter-Pounders with cheese.

Pa Ingalls wouldn't believe his eyes.

Moving from a muscle society to a mental society

7

caught the family off guard. Revolutions in information, transportation, and mechanization have cost us dearly. Our sense of permanence, unity, and peace are being jeopardized by our hurried lifestyles. The family that makes it through life without bearing the marks of a hurried home is the exception, not the rule.

Over the past fifteen years I've watched the speed at which we live our lives go from second gear to *overdrive*. In counseling individuals and couples across the country, I've observed at least six characteristics that mark hurried families. Separately they're bad. Combine them and they're deadly. They attack the faith, joy, and love needed for a family to be at rest.

Let's take a brief look at six families, each illustrating one of the characteristics of a hurried home.

THE BAILEYS: CAN'T RELAX

Meet the Baileys . . . if you can. It's hard to get to know them because their schedule doesn't allow much time to cultivate close friends. But they do have a lot of acquaintances. They meet them through the numerous "projects" and activities that make up their day.

The Baileys are the envy of the neighborhood. On the surface they look ideal, but their industrious veneer hides one of the standard marks of a hurried family. They can't relax.

It's not that they *don't* relax; it's that they *can't* relax. What some would describe as resourcefulness is just a cover-up for restlessness.

The Baileys aren't bad, they're just too busy.

THE GRAHAMS: CAN'T ENJOY QUIET

The Grahams' house is always filled with sound. It's hard to tell exactly what the music is, however, because of the different strains emanating from different rooms.

Between the compact discs and televisions blaring, it's hard to get a thought in edge-wise. When they sit down to dinner, they find out more about the cast of Cosby's day than their own. The Grahams can't enjoy quiet; they are intimidated by silence.

As their hearts cry out for rest, they answer back with entertainment. By keeping their brains occupied with external sounds, they don't have to face the emptiness within. Noise is the Valium that helps the Grahams cope with inner restlessness.

THE JONESES: NEVER FEEL SATISFIED

The Joneses are the ones everyone is trying to keep up with. They have everything money can buy, but tragically, the Joneses are never satisfied. They aren't satisfied with what they have, where they live, or what they are.

For this family, contentment is always just around the corner—in the latest shipment from L. L. Bean, in being the first one on their block to have one. One *what?* It doesn't really matter, as long as they're first. They are a family robbed of rest, because they have failed to see that satisfaction is a choice.

THE GARDNERS: AN ABSENCE OF ABSOLUTES

The only thing you can be certain of with the Gardners is their uncertainty. They display an astonishing lack of permanence in their family—and have a hard time imagining life beyond the moment.

Their home is a collection of unfinished projects, cluttered with unneeded items bought on impulse and in bad need of repair. They are great at starting but poor at finishing . . . at pursuing ideas without a plan . . . at searching but never finding . . . at consistently confusing yes and no.

It hurts to watch the restless, wandering Gardners. They refuse to recognize an absolute authority in their lives, so they never feel sure of themselves. They go to church and occasionally read the Bible, but they are not convicted by it enough to let it guide them in specific decisions. They are restless because they live for the immediate at the expense of the permanent.

THE MOORES: MISGUIDED SERVANTHOOD

The Moores are great people who do wonderful things for others, but they are unhappy. Why? Because they do good things for the wrong reasons. Their sympathetic gift is more often a cover-up for their own need for affirmation. They crave approval. They need to hear the compliments in order to convince themselves that they are valuable.

We all love the Moores. At some time or another, we all *need* the Moores. But we don't want to *be* the Moores. Their struggle for approval makes us tired. They are marked as a hurried family because they don't know how to handle their insecurities. They are denied rest by their inordinate need to be liked.

THE EVANSES: "WORLD CLASS" OVER-ACHIEVERS
The Evanses aren't able to rest because they don't know how to lose. Theirs is a love affair with winning. They are happy *only* when they are succeeding. But because success is always temporary, they push themselves and their children from one victory to the next. Their laurel leaves wither on their restless heads. They are a family with much pride and little joy. Their home suffers because they have failed to appropriate the keys to genuine rest. *(Adapted from chapters 1 and 2 of* Little House on the Freeway.*)*

PERSONAL REFLECTION
The Marks of the Hurried Family
  • Can't relax
  • Can't enjoy quiet
  • Seldom feel satisfied
  • Lack absolutes
  • Serve for wrong reasons
  • Motivated by over-achievement

1. Of the six marks of the hurried family, which one(s) best describes your home? Why?

▶**2.** Being hurried is a conditioning that we receive from the constant pressure of our culture. We are a society that highly values a hurried lifestyle. Using the following areas as a checklist, what are some ways that you are pushed to speed up your life at the expense of genuine calm?

- Media
- Education
- Workplace
- Church

▶**3.** Has the hurried lifestyle caused you to think more about internal rest? If so, in what ways?

REST IN JESUS
"Come to me, all you who are weary and burdened, and I will give you rest. Take my yoke upon you and learn from me, for I am gentle and humble in heart, and you will find rest for your souls. For my yoke is easy and my burden is light." (Matthew 11:28-30)

4. Jesus gave three commands in Matthew 11:28-30. What are we told to do?

5. What promise accompanies these commands?

6. What do you think it means to come to Jesus in this context?

7. a. A yoke harnesses two oxen together to plow as a team. In the day when Jesus shared this truth, the yoke was tailor-made for the neck and shoulders of the particular oxen that would use it. What do you suppose it means to take on Jesus' yoke?

    b. What yokes (besides the one attached to Jesus) do you feel bound to today?

    c. How do you think being yoked together with Christ could make the hurried lifestyle more bearable?

8. Jesus tells us to learn from Him. How can you make yourself available to Him for this learning process?

9. What do you think gentleness and humility have to do with finding rest?

LOOKING TO GOD

If you have never responded to Jesus' invitation to come to Him to find eternal rest for your soul, then consider making that decision now. The invitation is for everyone. No one who responds is excluded for any reason.

INTO OUR LIVES

Learning from Jesus won't happen by accident, and countering the effects of the hurried lifestyle requires a deliberate plan. Since rest begins by assuming a yoked position with Christ, let's look at some specific things that we can do this week to begin the process of making God's daily rest a part of our schedule. Take a few minutes to decide, as individuals or couples, what steps you will take during the following week. Choose one of the following suggestions, or make your own plan. Then tell one other member of your group what you've decided.

1. Spend some time as a couple or family evaluating your pace of life. (Are you content with your present lifestyle? Do you spend enough time together? What are some of the negative effects of a hurried lifestyle that are hurting your relationship as a family?)

2. Set the alarm to go off fifteen minutes earlier this week. Find a place in your home to have a daily appointment with God. Read a chapter a day from the Gospel of John. Ask the Lord to show you what He wants you to be learning from Him at this time in your life. Ask God to help you stay yoked to Him.

3. Memorize Matthew 11:28-30. (See page 11.) Write down any thoughts you have about these verses as you meditate on them.

4. Keep a piece of paper in your Bible this week. Each evening, review your day. List the times when you were hurrying and the reason for the rush. Look for a pattern. What changes can you make to be less hurried?

5. Renew your commitment to walk with Jesus and sur-render your whole life to Him. Set aside a special time and place to renew your fellowship with Him. Ask Him to help you be more consistent in heeding His call to come to Him, to plow with Him, and to learn from Him.

6. Read and reflect on the quotes in the "For Meditation" section. Talk with God about what these insights mean for your life.

FOR MEDITATION

Being hurried comes naturally; while being at rest requires an ongoing appraisal of priorities. All of us who are serious about our spiritual life and our family life must counter the forces threatening our ability to maintain rest.

Tim Kimmel

The Lord doesn't want the first place in my life; He wants all of my life.

Howard Armerding

Our Lord did not teach detachment from other things: He taught attachment to Himself.

Oswald Chambers
So Send I You

It has been well said that no man ever sank under the burden of the day. It is when tomorrow's burden is added to the burden of today that the weight is more than a man can bear. Never load yourselves so, my friends. If you find yourselves so loaded, at least remember this: it is your own doing, not God's. He begs you to leave the future to Him, and mind the present.

George MacDonald

Each morning is a new beginning of our life. Each day is a finished whole. The present day marks the boundary of our cares and concerns (Matthew 6:34, James 4:14). It is long enough to find God or to lose him, to keep faith or fall into disgrace. Every morning God gives us the gift of compre-hending anew his faithfulness of old; thus, in the midst of

14

our life with God we may daily begin a new life with him.

Dietrich Bonhoeffer
Meditating on the Word

Look around and be distressed; look within and be depressed; look at Jesus and be at rest.

Corrie ten Boom

Busyness rapes relationships. It substitutes shallow frenzy for deep friendship. It promises satisfying dreams, but delivers hollow nightmares. It feeds the ego, but starves the inner man. It fills the calendar but fractures the family. It cultivates a program, but plows under priorities.

Charles Swindoll
Killing Giants, Pulling Thorns

The Foundation for Genuine Rest

WARM-UP
• Share with the group what you learned during the past week about being yoked to Jesus and finding rest in Him.
• When you think of the word *rest*, what comes to your mind? Share your ideas.

GRACE FOR OUR NEEDS

❝ At the foundation of human rest are three inner needs. We build our lives on and around them. They are powerful needs that demand satisfaction, and are as essential to our survival as food, clothing, and shelter. If they are met in legitimate, healthy ways, our lives can experience a sweet contentment. Deny yourself any or all of these needs, and you will put into place all of the necessary ingredients for a restless life.

Just as the various hues of the rainbow are shades of three primary colors, the complexities that make up life are only variations of three inner needs. *Love, purpose,* and *hope* are what everyone needs to feel complete.

ACCEPTANCE: THE NEED FOR LOVE
There is probably no greater inner pain than the pain of loneliness. Our culture might have popularized the cult of self-worship, but it is an empty shrine. We can make macho speeches, or play self-sufficient games, but our independent attitude is a thin veneer at best. Deep within every living soul is a gnawing need to be accepted.

We are made so by design. God put a perfect man in

a perfect environment—yet Adam was lonely. Fashioned to be incomplete by himself, his heart longed for companionship. It was because of his longing that God made a woman for him to love. Eve completed a heart that was meant to be bonded with another.

"Love is a two-way street," croons the Country and Western singer, "but my baby's changing lanes." A healthy person never gets good at being jilted. The thousandth time you've been rejected hurts just as deeply as the first. So fundamental is man's need for love that some people have died for lack of it. *Marasmus* is the clinical expression, but the layman's dictionary would define it as simply "lack of love."

AFFIRMATION: THE NEED FOR PURPOSE

Love is a driving need that gives security, but we need purpose to feel significant. We need that little spark of attention from someone who believes in us. The mileage that the human spirit can derive from an affirming word is endless.

Most achievers fall into two categories. They either have a purpose and are motivated to live it out, or they are madly driven to find one. Innate within the concept of rest is a confidence that you are significant.

Andor Foldes, a gifted classical musician, struggled with affirmation early in his career. The first affirming word he recalls was at age seven when his father kissed him and thanked him for helping in the garden. He remembers it over *six decades later,* as though it were yesterday. But another kiss changed his life.

At age sixteen, living in Budapest, Foldes was already a skilled pianist. But he was at his personal all-time low because of a conflict with his piano teacher. In the midst of that very troubled year, however, one of the most renowned pianists of the day came to the city to perform. Emil von Sauer was not only famous because of his abilities at the piano, but he could also claim the notoriety of being the last surviving pupil of Franz Liszt.

Sauer requested that young Foldes play for him. Foldes obliged the master with some of the most difficult works of Bach, Beethoven, and Schumann. When he finished, Sauer walked over to him and kissed him on the forehead.

"My son," he said, "when I was your age I became a student of Liszt. He kissed me on the forehead after my first lesson, saying, 'Take good care of this kiss—it comes from Beethoven, who gave it to me after hearing me play.' I have waited for years to pass on this sacred heritage, but now I feel you deserve it."[1]

Foldes no longer had a personal crisis. His kiss from Beethoven gave him a new sense of purpose.

ASSURANCE: THE NEED FOR HOPE

The trilogy of our inner needs is not complete without hope. Hope is the environment in which love and purpose breed contentment. It is the third strand that gives strength to our security and significance.

What good is it if you are making great time on a road to nowhere? Too many people are confused into thinking that a kind word and a sense of direction are enough. But hope is the glimmer of light of the horizon that says there is a reason to keep moving forward. The light might be faint and the road long, but the trip is bearable if we are certain there is a destination.

Hopes and dreams are often used as synonyms. In the Cinderella world that too many people live in, living happily ever after is followed by waking up to reality. Hope has to be more than that.

If dreams are made of sand, then hope is made of concrete. It's the bulkhead that withstands the pounding waves of life's stormy seas. It's the belief in the back of our minds that assures our spirits. But it must have a divine touch to last. Hope that is a product of human intuition is temporal. Those who allow God's love to cast its cross-shaped shadow over their human spirit give hope eternal life.

THERE IS PEACE

The pressures that create restless spirits can be countered by the elements of genuine rest. But these external solutions assume that we first have accepted God's internal solutions.

He loves us.

He made us with a purpose.

He guarantees us hope.

Rest is an attitude based on truth that we're certain of, regardless of the doubts. It's a deposit that our mind makes to the accounts of our hearts when we know the pressures aren't going to be quickly removed. We claim it more often and exercise it more regularly when we view it as a strategy for persevering, rather than an escape hatch.

(Adapted from chapter 3 of Little House on the Freeway.*)*

LOVE

"O LORD . . . how priceless is your unfailing love!"

(Psalm 36:6-7)

1. On the scale below, indicate how well the people in your life (parents, other family members, friends, lovers) have succeeded in making you feel deeply loved.

1	2	3	4	5	6	7	8	9	10
Total failure									Total success

"You see, at just the right time, when we were still powerless, Christ died for the ungodly. Very rarely will anyone die for a righteous man, though for a good man someone might possibly dare to die. But God demonstrates his own love for us in this: While we were still sinners, Christ died for us." (Romans 5:6-8)

"He who did not spare his own Son, but gave him up for us all—how will he not also, along with him, graciously give us all things? Who will bring any charge against those whom God has chosen? It is God who justifies. Who is he that condemns? Christ Jesus, who died—more than that, who was raised to life—is at the right hand of God and is also interceding for us. Who shall separate us from the love of Christ? Shall trouble or hardship or persecu-

tion or famine or nakedness or danger or sword? As it is
written:

"'For your sake we face death all day long;
we are considered as sheep to be slaughtered.'
No, in all these things we are more than conquerors
through him who loved us. For I am convinced that
neither death nor life, neither angels nor demons,
neither the present nor the future, nor any powers,
neither height nor depth, nor anything else in all crea-
tion, will be able to separate us from the love of God that
is in Christ Jesus our Lord." (Romans 8:32-39)

2. According to Romans 5:6-8 and 8:32-39, how has God
demonstrated that He loves you deeply and securely?

We often feel unloved and lonely because we focus
more on people's rejection than on God's acceptance. God's overflowing love seems to matter less
than how people treat us.

3. Do you tend to act as though *God's* love or *people's* love
matters more to you? Why do you suppose that is?

PURPOSE
"'Love the Lord your God with all your heart and with all
your soul and with all your mind.' This is the first and
greatest commandment. And the second is like it: 'Love
your neighbor as yourself.' All the Law and the Prophets
hang on these two commandments." (Matthew 22:37-40)

4. As Christians, our lives are filled with purpose that comes from God. According to Jesus words in Matthew 22:37-40, what should be the primary goals of our lives?

"We know, brothers, that God not only loves you but has selected you for a special purpose." (1 Thessalonians 1:4, PH)

"You became imitators of us and of the Lord; in spite of severe suffering, you welcomed the message with the joy given by the Holy Spirit. And so you became a model to all the believers in Macedonia and Achaia. The Lord's message rang out from you not only in Macedonia and Achaia—your faith in God has become known everywhere." (1 Thessalonians 1:6-8)

5. Read 1 Thessalonians 1:4,6-8. What did the Thessalonians do in response to Paul's message about their purpose?

6. If these were the consuming purposes of your life, how would your way of life be different?

Think About It:
What specific purpose or calling does God have for you at this time of your life?

HOPE
"For you have been my hope, O Sovereign LORD."
(Psalm 71:5)

The New Testament idea of hope is different from the hope we express when we say, "I hope I get that job." It means "something we confidently expect." It involves enduring and overcoming as we wait patiently for what we expect.

"Then I saw a new heaven and a new earth, for the first heaven and the first earth had passed away, and there was no longer any sea. I saw the Holy City, the new Jerusalem, coming down out of heaven from God, prepared as a bride beautifully dressed for her husband. And I heard a loud voice from the throne saying, 'Now the dwelling of God is with men, and he will live with them. They will be his people, and God himself will be with them and be their God. He will wipe every tear from their eyes. There will be no more death or mourning or crying or pain, for the old order of things has passed away.'

"He who was seated on the throne said, 'I am making everything new! . . .

"'It is done. I am the Alpha and the Omega, the Beginning and the End. To him who is thirsty I will give to drink without cost from the spring of the water of life. He who overcomes will inherit all this, and I will be his God and he will be my son.'" (Revelation 21:1-7)

7. Read Revelation 21:1-7.

    a. What is the Christians' hope? What do we confidently expect? (If time allows, see also Romans 8:18-25.)

    b. How do you think this hope should affect the way you deal with life?

c. What seem to be the chief barriers that block you from staying focused on your hope?

For Further Investigation:
How do the New Testament writers say our hope should affect the way we live? (See 2 Corinthians 4:6–5:10, Hebrews 11:1–12:12.)

LOOKING TO GOD
Divide into groups of three. Tell the other members of your triad which of the three needs—love, purpose, or hope—seems to be the biggest gap in your life right now. Tell them briefly why you chose that need. Then pray for each other, that God would enable you to become secure in His love, confident in His purpose for you, or focused on the hope set before you. Pray also for any other personal concerns.

INTO OUR LIVES
Select one of the following responses to what you've learned in this session, or plan one of your own. Then tell the other members of your triad what you plan to do.

1. Choose one of the following passages to meditate on this week: Romans 8:23-25, 2 Corinthians 4:16-18, 1 Thessalonians 1:4, 1 John 3:1. Write it on a 3 x 5 card, and put the card where you will see it often (a bathroom mirror, the refrigerator, etc.). Use this passage to remind you that God can meet your need for love, purpose, or hope.

2. Decide on a specific action you could take this week to demonstrate God's love, share God's hope, or help someone find God's purpose. For example: you could take a meal to a senior, write a note of encouragement to each of your children, or offer to have a time of prayer with a friend who is struggling to know God's will.

3. As a group, find a way to express God's love to someone. Plan to offer to do household chores for an elderly couple, help a family move, or have a group garage sale and then use the money for a missionary project or a needy family.

4. Make a date to meet with someone else in your group. Over lunch, coffee, or whatever, explore more deeply what keeps each of you from resting in God's love, purpose, or hope. Then pray for each other.

FOR MEDITATION

I once more realized that the ways of the Lord are imponderable. That we ourselves never know what we want. And how many times in life I passionately sought what I did not need and have been despondent over failures that were successes.

Aleksandr Solzhenitsyn

God made thee to love Him, and not to understand Him.

Voltaire

Thou has made us for Thyself, and the heart of man is restless until it finds its rest in Thee.

Augustine

It is impossible for that man to despair who remembers that his helper is omnipotent.

Jeremy Taylor

Human life stands in desperate need of courage: the conviction that life will not only continue, but triumph. Without such basic assurance—a reserve of confidence and hope—life withers away, paralyzed by despair.

Klaus Bockmuehl

Man, made in the image of God, has a purpose—to be in relationship to God, who is there. Man forgets his purpose

and thus he forgets who he is and what life means.
Francis A. Schaeffer

Our only business is to love God, and delight ourselves in Him.
Brother Lawrence
The Practice of the Presence of God

NOTE
1. Andor Foldes, "Beethoven's Kiss," *Reader's Digest* (November 1986), page 145.

A Forgiving Spirit

WARM-UP

- Share what you learned this past week about finding or demonstrating God's love, purpose, or hope.
- Think of a recent time when you were hurt by someone. Recall your immediate response. How hard is it now for you to forgive that person? Where do you belong on this scale?

1	2	3	4	5	6	7	8	9	10

I have no intention of forgiving.   I have completely forgiven.

The goal of enjoying rest in our lives must be approached from two perspectives. First, we must bring rest to our souls. Second, we must make changes in our day-to-day habits. In the next few sessions, we will look at the steps we must take to bring calm and confidence to our spirits. We'll deal with the first essential in this session.

Rest, in our stressful and demanding culture, is found in embracing a handful of fundamentals. Rest is not restricted to the experts in time management, or those fortunate enough to enjoy large chunks of discretionary time. Rest belongs to those willing to continually maintain a few basic requirements.

THE FIRST NECESSITY FOR REST: WE MUST FORGIVE

As I study the Bible, I am impressed by the recurring themes that separate the rested heart from the restless. Those who have discovered rest seem to share at

27

least six characteristics that set them apart. These characteristics grow out of non-negotiable principles—essential if you want to enjoy a calm and rested spirit on an on-going basis.

The first necessity for rest is that we maintain an attitude of forgiveness. A person unwilling or unable to forgive can never be at rest.

As deeply as we may long for peace and rest, many of us find the corridors of our hearts haunted by ghosts from the past. Walking corpses. Grotesque, bitter spirits that moan and linger and rattle their chains—because we have refused to forgive people who have done us wrong.

The degree that you and I are open to experiencing inner rest is equally proportionate to our willingness to forgive and be forgiven. Some of you reading these words need not search any further to find out why you are not experiencing inner rest.

Unresolved conflict, cutting words, cruel rumors, and the isolation of your heart because of rejection siphon the joy away from even the most beautiful moments of life. The rest that you long for runs ahead of you—like a rainbow, forever out of reach.

We all have some hurt that loves to come back and steal our joy. It sits in the back of our memory waiting for an opportunity to be recalled. It's always there, and no matter how hard we try, we can't remove it. There are myriad of advantages to being human rather than a computer, but sometimes it would be nice to have all of our painful memories stored on a floppy disc stuck in the side of our head. A simple command could erase the hurt.

Even though we can't erase the hurts that lie stored in the file drawers of our memory, we *can* offset their negative impact. In chemistry, if I want to neutralize an acid, I must counter with the equivalent of an opposite substance. Forgiveness works like that. It's an alkaline nullifying the acidic nature of bitterness. It's that balancing presence that says "You can remind me of my pain, but you can't rob me of my rest."

If we don't deal with our unresolved conflicts, they'll deal with us. Bitterness is a slavemaster. It controls us. It demands too much.

I've had the same choices that face all people. I could be haunted and hounded by hurt, or I could forgive. If I make the choice to forgive, it is not because of some intrinsic good in me. I'm just as capable of revenge as the next guy. My decision to forgive is more motivated by need and desperation.

When the crimes against my heart seem unforgivable, I am compelled to take a walk up a hill. Hurting hearts all over the world have learned the power that is gained by taking this same walk. The Hill of Forgiveness sits at the center of civilization. The ground at the top is level. The grass growing around the wooden beam with its crossbeam ripples in the fresh breeze of freedom. There's always room for anyone wanting help for their hurt.

The cross is the single most significant symbol of forgiveness in history. Made by men, used by God, it is the hallmark of man at his worst and God at His best.

God paid for man with outstretched arms. He no longer hangs on the cross, but His arms are in the same position. Because of Him, I'm forgiven in spite of myself. He receives the guilty. He welcomes the wounded.

None of us deserves this kind of forgiveness. It's a gift. Once you've received it, it's impossible to remain the same.

We want rest. But it will cost us. The menu for rest lists a lot of variations of "humble pie." But if pride is going to hold us hostage, we'll find that we are our own worst enemy. Maybe now is a good time for you to do a serious inventory of your life. Are there people whom you need to forgive? Do yourself a favor. Give them something they don't deserve but desperately need. Give them the gift of forgiveness. It's a gift that, once given, offers something in return. Your spirit gets a rest.

(Adapted from chapter 4 of Little House on the Freeway.*)*

LEARNING TO FORGIVE

"Then Peter came to Jesus and asked, 'Lord, how many times shall I forgive my brother when he sins against me?

Up to seven times?'

"Jesus answered, 'I tell you, not seven times, but seventy-seven times.

"'Therefore, the kingdom of heaven is like a king who wanted to settle accounts with his servants. As he began the settlement, a man who owed him ten thousand talents was brought to him. Since he was not able to pay, the master ordered that he and his wife and his children and all that he had be sold to repay the debt.

"'The servant fell on his knees before him. "Be patient with me," he begged, "and I will pay back everything." The servant's master took pity on him, canceled the debt and let him go.

"'But when that servant went out, he found one of his fellow servants who owed him a hundred denarii. He grabbed him and began to choke him. "Pay back what you owe me!" he demanded.

"'His fellow servant fell to his knees and begged him, "Be patient with me, and I will pay you back."

"'But he refused. Instead, he went off and had the man thrown into prison until he could pay the debt. When the other servants saw what had happened, they were greatly distressed and went and told their master everything that had happened.

"'Then the master called the servant in. "You wicked servant," he said, "I canceled all that debt of yours because you begged me to. Shouldn't you have had mercy on your fellow servant just as I had on you?" In anger his master turned him over to the jailers to be tortured, until he should pay back all he owed.

"'This is how my heavenly Father will treat each of you unless you forgive your brother from your heart.'" (Matthew 18:21-35)

1. Read Matthew 18:21-35. What is the *point* made in this parable?

▶**2.** Do you find the unforgiving servant's behavior normal or astonishing? Why?

3. Why do you suppose this servant was unwilling to forgive? (Suggest as many reasons as you can.)

4. a. Complete this sentence: "It's tough for me to forgive when . . . ."

  b. Why do these factors make it hard to forgive someone? (For instance, how is pride involved? What about fear?)

5. Are the following statements true or false biblically?

T F Forgiveness means that what the person did was okay.

T F Forgiveness means the person can do the same thing again.

T F Forgiveness means I won't dwell on the event.

T F Forgiveness means I won't feel hurt anymore.

T F Forgiveness means I renounce the right to get revenge.

T F Forgiveness means I won't withdraw love in order to protect myself.

6. Do you find it easier to forgive yourself or others? Why do you think this is the case?

"Do not repay anyone evil for evil. Be careful to do what is right in the eyes of everybody. If it is possible, as far as it depends on you, live at peace with everyone. Do not take revenge, my friends, but leave room for God's wrath, for it is written: 'It is mine to avenge; I will repay,' says the Lord. On the contrary: 'If your enemy is hungry, feed him; if he is thirsty, give him something to drink. In doing this, you will heap burning coals on his head.' Do not be overcome by evil, but overcome evil with good." (Romans 12:17-21)

7. a. What does Paul say in Romans 12:17-21 about the place of revenge?

   b. Why is it better that God be left with the responsibility of revenge?

STEPS TO FORGIVENESS

8. Read through the following steps to forgiveness. Think of any situations where the process of forgiveness remains incomplete for you.

- *Talk* to God. Tell Him how you feel. It may help to write down the offense and the reasons why you are hurt.
- *Confess* your own sin. Ask the Lord to help you with your pride and unwillingness to forgive.
- *Choose* to forgive. Let go of your own interests and forgive.
- *Ask* God to give you His love and forgiveness.
- *Trust* in God's justice. God will deal in His own time and in His own way with the person who wronged you.
- *Remember* that God is able to keep you free from bitterness. If unforgiving thoughts recur, memorize a Scripture verse that deals with forgiveness, and think

about it whenever you feel unforgiving. (Consider Luke 17:3-4, Romans 12:18-21, Ephesians 4:31-32, Colossians 3:13, and 1 Peter 1:23.)

• *Discuss* the offense with the person who wronged you, if possible. (This may not be possible or even advisable.) Ask the Lord to show you whether this would be the best action to take. You may want to seek counsel from a mature and trustworthy Christian friend, but be careful not to gossip about the offense.

• *Thank* the Lord for taking you through this humbling process. You will grow in humility, mercy, and meekness as you learn to forgive, especially when it's difficult.

Which steps do you most often have trouble with?

▶**9.** Ask a group member to describe what he or she experienced after letting go of a hurt and truly forgiving another.

10. Who is hurt more when you fail to forgive—the person who has wronged you, or you? Why is this so?

11. Do you agree that failing to forgive deprives us of rest? Why do you think this is the case?

INTO OUR LIVES
1. Spend time alone this week making a list of people you have not completely forgiven. Apply the steps to forgiveness for each item you have listed. Write your thoughts in

the form of a prayer to God. Be sure to memorize a verse of your choice for the "remember" step.

2. If your struggle is more with forgiving yourself, examine the reasons. Have you failed to repent and turn from the sin you feel guilty about? Are you holding on to a feeling of guilt as a way of "paying" for your sin? As you think about these questions, write down your thoughts.

Spend time reflecting on God's forgiveness. When we refuse to forgive ourselves, we are making light of the price Jesus Christ paid to purchase our forgiveness. Ask Him to help you let go of your guilt and embrace His forgiveness. Memorize one of the following verses to remind you that Jesus paid the price and that you are forgiven: Romans 5:8, 2 Corinthians 5:21, Ephesians 1:7.

FOR MEDITATION
Forgiveness is man's deepest need and highest achievement.
Horace Bushnell

He that cannot forgive others breaks the bridge over which he must pass himself; for every man has need to be forgiven.
Thomas Fuller

There's no point in burying a hatchet if you're going to put up a marker on the site.
Sydney Harris

Only one petition in the Lord's prayer has any condition attached to it; it is the petition for forgiveness.
William Temple

God does forgive, but it cost the rending of His heart in the death of Christ to enable Him to do so. The great miracle of the grace of God is that He forgives sin, and it is the death of Jesus Christ alone that enables the Divine nature to forgive and to remain true to itself in doing so.
Oswald Chambers
My Utmost for His Highest

Living Within the Limits

WARM-UP

• Let anyone who wants to recite the verse about forgiveness he or she chose to memorize.

Afterward, give everyone a chance to briefly share what happened when he or she went through the steps of forgiveness after last week's session. Did anyone in the group experience liberation from an old bitterness or guilt? If so, how has that affected that person's life? Or, did anyone learn something from memorizing the verse?

• Go around the room, letting each person respond to this question: "How do you generally feel about rules?"

a. I hate rules. They make me feel stifled. I rebel.

b. I love them. I feel insecure if I don't know the rules in every situation.

c. I like broad guidelines within which I am widely free to make choices and take risks.

d. I don't pay much attention to rules.

e. I like making rules for others, but I don't like following them when others make them.

f. I like rules for dealing with things (cooking, engineering, job situations, etc.), but I don't like rules for dealing with people.

g. I don't like rules, because although I am careful to follow them, it seems as though other people get away with ignoring them.

h. other (name it)

THE SECOND NECESSITY FOR REST: WE MUST LIVE OUR LIVES WITHIN THE BOUNDARIES OF GOD'S WORD

" So many of the people approaching me for counseling want relief without reprimand. They want to find
solutions to their inner restlessness, but don't want to
change their lifestyle. They want to feel the peace of God
while living in direct opposition to the stated principles of
His Scriptures. In short, they want the freedom to live life
outside the protective fence of God's Word—yet with the
gate left open so they can rush back inside and avoid any
negative consequences for their actions.

A funny thing happened on the way to the twenty-
first century. We decided that the concept of sin was
something we should leave behind as archaic and out-
of-date. While we were busy locating the elusive self
inside of us, we decided that guilt was too painful. The
only solution was to change the rules and "redefine"
wrong.

Where does this epidemic of hypocrisy and shifting
standards leave us? Without exception, it leads to the
wilderness of unrest. How can we return to the place
where right is right, and wrong is not excused on the
basis of our feelings? By following a narrow way marked
off by an eternal Book—a pathway that offers freedom
and rest by giving us the choice to live life within the
standards of God's Word.

Throughout Scripture and throughout the ages,
those who have entered into God's rest have done so by
making a conscious choice to stay within the protective
fence of God's standards. Put another way, the further we
walk away from biblical guidelines, the closer we get to

the cliffs of anxiety, fear, worry, and unrest.

While we may never have thought of it this way
before, one of the greatest gifts God has given us is the
ability to experience and feel guilt. While Freud and
others have called it the "universal neurosis"—a destruc-
tive force in people's lives—it can actually be something
God uses to protect us.

I'm not saying that all guilt is good. Imaginary guilt,
or guilt imposed on us by people wanting to control us, is
false and damaging. True guilt, however, serves us spiritually the way fever serves us physically. When we get a
fever, our body is telling our mind that we have a sickness
somewhere. A person who wants to get better doesn't
ignore his symptoms. Neither does he hate himself
because he's feeling sick. Rather, the negative feelings act
as a physical reminder that the fence has been crossed
between sickness and health.

In the same way guilt tells us that something is
wrong with us emotionally or spiritually. It says in a clear
way, *You're stepping outside the fence by making this decision
. . . pursuing this relationship . . . avoiding this person . . .
accepting this invitation. . . .*

Here's the bottom line regarding this element of
rest: We need to align our actions with our beliefs. In so
doing, we acknowledge that there is a protective fence
God has put around our behavior. We honor Him, we
honor our loved ones, and we honor ourselves by
respecting it.

We give our family, friends, and ourselves an incredible gift when we make the decision to live within God's
limits. It opens the door to genuine rest in our lives, and
perhaps even more importantly, it models the pathway to
rest that they can follow in theirs.

(Adapted from chapter 5 of Little House on the Freeway.*)*

BENEFITS OF LIVING WITHIN GOD'S GUIDELINES

"Jesus said, 'If you hold to my teaching, you are really my
disciples. Then you will know the truth, and the truth will
set you free. . . . Everyone who sins is a slave to sin. Now
a slave has no permanent place in the family, but a son

belongs to it forever. So if the Son sets you free, you will be free indeed.'" (John 8:31-32,34-36)

In this passage, Jesus says that truth sets us free. But by definition, truth is confining; it is nonnegotiable. The biblical idea of truth includes not just ideas, but also ethics and values—the true way to live.

1. How can knowing the true way to live set us free, even though it gives us boundaries? (By contrast, why is living without moral boundaries really slavery?)

We all live by rules. Can you imagine getting through a busy intersection where no one knew or cared about traffic laws or stoplights? Would you want to buy a house from someone who didn't believe in contracts? Have you ever tried to break the law of gravity by jumping off a cliff? You wouldn't break the law of gravity; you'd illustrate it.

God's rules are like that. A law like "You shall not commit adultery" is meant to protect us, just as traffic laws and contracts are. We can try to break laws like these, but we just end up illustrating the moral law of gravity: "A man reaps what he sows" (Galatians 6:7).

"The law of the LORD is perfect,
     reviving the soul.
The statutes of the LORD are trustworthy,
     making wise the simple.
The precepts of the LORD are right,
     giving joy to the heart.
The commands of the LORD are radiant,
     giving light to the eyes.
The fear of the LORD is pure,
     enduring forever.
The ordinances of the LORD are sure
     and altogether righteous.

They are more precious than gold,
     than much pure gold;
They are sweeter than honey,
     than honey from the comb.
By them is your servant warned;
     in keeping them there is great reward."

(Psalm 19:7-11)

▶**2.** Read Psalm 19:7-11. Why does the psalmist David regard God's guidelines as perfect, trustworthy, right, radiant, pure, sure, and precious?

"You, then, who teach others, do you not teach yourself? You who preach against stealing, do you steal? You who say that people should not commit adultery, do you commit adultery? You who abhor idols, do you rob temples? You who brag about the law, do you dishonor God by breaking the law? As it is written: 'God's name is blasphemed among the Gentiles because of you.'" (Romans 2:21-24)

"Do not be deceived: God cannot be mocked. A man reaps what he sows. The one who sows to please his sinful nature, from that nature will reap destruction; the one who sows to please the Spirit, from the Spirit will reap eternal life. Let us not become weary in doing good, for at the proper time we will reap a harvest if we do not give up." (Galatians 6:7-9)

3. Paul says that ignoring God's limits causes others to blaspheme His name (Romans 2:24) and causes us to reap the destruction we sow (Galatians 6:7-8). The following examples are of people trying to live by situational values instead of scriptural guidelines. Choose two or three of the examples to discuss.

- A mother is addicted to the most permissive of the daytime soaps, but preaches to her daughter about the questionable messages of rock-'n'-roll.
- A man goes on vacation with his family, but makes one "business" call in order to deduct the entire trip on his income taxes.
- A mother reprimands her child for lying to her, but consistently has the child tell a caller to whom she doesn't want to speak that she is not home.
- A father lectures his kids about their taste in movies, but rents adult videos for private viewing.
- An woman turns in a shoplifter, but outfits her desk at home with supplies she requisitioned at work.
- A service manager is outspoken against the use of bad language by his children, but is even more outspoken in his use of coarse language at work to "motivate" his men.
- A young woman knows all the verses about not marrying a nonChristian, but does it anyway because "it can't be wrong when it feels so right."
- A family is publicly committed to the pro-life cause, but decides their own teenage daughter's only option is to have an abortion.

What do you expect will be the consequences of situational values in these people's lives?

Think About It:
Think of a specific time when you compromised your beliefs by your actions. Were there any consequences? If so, what were they? At what point did you recognize that you were compromising? What happened to help you recognize that you were outside of God's limits?

40

The Apostle Paul's main theme in both Romans and Galatians is that Christians need to live by *faith* in God's grace, not by the law. That is, our confidence of pleasing God is not in our ability to keep the rules, but in His mercy and grace through Jesus Christ—forgiving our failures and transforming us into Christ's image. Neither Psalm 19 nor Romans 2 nor Galatians 6 teaches legalism—the idea that we earn God's approval by keeping the rules. We are enabled to obey God by His power, out of love for Him and others.

> *Grace:* God's empowering presence in us, enabling us to be what He calls us to be and to do what He calls us to do.
>
> James Ryle

PERSONAL REFLECTION

5. Take five minutes alone to read through and reflect on the following list of areas where God has clear standards, drawn from Colossians 3:1–4:6. Ask yourself, "Am I forfeiting God's rest by ignoring His guidelines in any of these areas?"

- setting your heart on earthly things, such as possessions, career, prestige;
- sexual immorality;
- looking at materials that encourage lust—movies, magazines;
- greed, coveting possessions;
- anger;
- slander—putting others down;
- gossip—talking about others behind their back;
- filthy language—swearing, nagging, yelling;
- lying;
- harshness with spouse or children;
- lack of submission;
- embittering children;
- slacking off at work, cheating;
- exploiting employees.

Write down the area(s) in which you think God is most concerned that you change.

LOOKING TO GOD

Pair up with one other person in your group. Tell him or her as much about the area(s) you named in question 5 as you feel comfortable revealing. Then take a couple of minutes to pray for each other. Ask for God's grace to deal with the areas you have each mentioned. Pray also about any other needs in one another's lives.

INTO OUR LIVES

During the next week, give some attention to the area(s) of compromise you identified in question 5 above. Select one or more of the following tactics for letting God uproot a bad habit from your life.

1. Identify the situations or relationships in your life that tend to cause you to compromise or step outside of God's limits. (For example: "Now that we have cable television, I often watch shows that make me think about sexual lust or angry violence." "When I spend time at the mall, I tend to want things I don't need." "When I'm around Sally a lot, I am influenced by her negative attitude.") Make a commitment to avoid or sufficiently modify those situations so that you are not drawn into your bad habit.

2. Have a serious talk with God about the boundaries you consistently find yourself crossing. Ask Him to expose and deal with your underlying attitudes. Ask Him for the grace to resist. Ask Him what you can do to gain the attitude David expressed in Psalm 19:7-11.

3. Seek out a friend, perhaps someone in your group, who will help keep you accountable in areas where you tend to compromise. Agree to get together or talk on the phone once a week for a few months. Pray for each other.

FOR MEDITATION

Men do not reject the Bible because it contradicts itself but because it contradicts them.

E. Paul Hovey

"False guilt" is what comes as a result of the judgments and suggestions of men. "True guilt" is what results from divine judgment.

Paul Tournier
Guilt and Grace

The Bible is an inexhaustible fountain of all truths. The existence of the Bible is the greatest blessing humanity has ever experienced.

Immanuel Kant

The Bible is alive, it speaks to me; it has feet, it runs after me; it has hands, it lays hold of me.

Martin Luther

If fifty million people say a foolish thing, it is still a foolish thing.

Anatole France

To know is not enough; we must apply. To will is not enough; we must do.

Goethe

An Eternal Perspective

WARM-UP
- Take a few minutes to report on what has happened since you committed yourselves to live within God's limits in certain areas.
- How much of the time would you say you have an eternal perspective on your life? Where would you place yourself on this scale?

1	2	3	4	5	6	7	8	9	10

I'm always caught up in the temporal.   The things of God are my constant focus.

THE THIRD NECESSITY FOR REST:
WE MUST LIVE AGAINST THE BACKDROP OF ETERNITY

❝ Everything in life takes on a different perspective when weighed against eternity. Relationships, accomplishments, and disappointments assume significant new meanings.

Life is both temporal *and* eternal. The day-to-day events that bring wrinkles to our foreheads, smiles to our faces, or tears to our eyes have a right to an immediate response. Whether we skin our knees, wound our spirits, or break our hearts, the emotions of the moment need to be felt.

Winning the Little League championship calls for celebration, and being cut from this year's cheerleading squad might require sackcloth and ashes. Nothing is gained by reminding your child that "as far as eternity

45

goes, the outcome of the game is meaningless." Nor does the counsel that "when you're dead and gone no one will remember who was on the cheerleading squad anyway" do anything but demonstrate an appalling lack of sensitivity.

An absurd preoccupation with the "sweet by and by" makes us of little value to people living in the "nasty now and now." Nonetheless, *we are eternal people.* Because we are, it would be equally absurd to ignore the obvious impact of our eternal nature. The soul that shares the body lives beyond the tomb. Its eternal destination has a timely influence on our day-to-day perspective.

So much of the key to rest is wrapped up in our *perspective.* That's why seeing ourselves against an eternal backdrop is so critical. If forgiveness gives us the ability to love, and clear boundaries a crystallized purpose, an eternal perspective gives us hope.

So many of the disappointments in people's lives come because they fail to factor in the eternal. Without a regular reminder that "This world is not my home, I'm just passing through," it's hard to enjoy contentment. We are forced to evaluate everything happening to us by arbitrary and superficial standards. Self-worth becomes an issue of achievement. Satisfaction becomes an issue of acquisition. Without the eternal, I'm in competition with the best the world can put forth rather than the best that lies within me.

Life without an eternal perspective trades living for longing, exchanges happiness for hurriedness, and gives up rest for restlessness. When this life is all that we've got going for us, we're forced to grab all the gusto we can. As fast as we can.

But once upon a time, an eternal God decided to give man a rest. It was an invitation to slow down and last longer. The price tag was high, but the end result was worth it for Him. He gave up something in order to win. He knew that living would first require dying, but that death would be the gateway to Eternity.

So God who once slept in a manger climbed up on a cross. He paid the price for inner rest. He took the shame, the guilt, and the punishment for our sins. He took care of the one problem that all men share in common—their lost condition.

But His Word makes it clear that dying wasn't enough. On Sunday morning when the stone that sealed Jesus in His crypt was supernaturally rolled back, the morning light crept across the floor and up the ledge to a pile of graveclothes.

Jesus vacated the grave in order to invade our hearts. Without the resurrection of Christ, there is only man-made hope. The message of the cross takes us beyond this life to eternal life. Those who embrace this truth are given the assurance that life on earth is just the beginning—a dress rehearsal.

The best is yet to come.

(Adapted from chapter 6 of Little House on the Freeway.*)*

AN ETERNAL PERSPECTIVE
CHANGES THE WAY WE VIEW PEOPLE

"Two sparrows are sold for a farthing, aren't they? Yet not a single sparrow falls to the ground without your father's knowledge. The very hairs of your head are all numbered. Never be afraid, then—you are far more valuable than sparrows." (Matthew 10:30, PH)

1. According to Jesus' statements in Matthew 10:30, how does God's perspective on people differ from the world's perspective?

2. People without an eternal perspective often try to substitute other things for good relationships with people. What are some of the things they try to substitute?

3. Describe a recent time when you had to choose between investing in a relationship and pursuing worldly gain. Which did you choose, and why? (For example: "I had to choose whether to read a story to my child or to start a new project on the house. I chose [the story, or the project] because . . . .")

AN ETERNAL PERSPECTIVE
CHANGES THE WAY WE VIEW LOVE
"When you did it to these brothers you were doing it to me." (Matthew 25:40, TLB)

4. If you could constantly keep the perspective that whatever you do to another person you are doing to Jesus Himself, how would your life change?

5. The friendships you have with people who have trusted Christ for their salvation are eternal friendships. You will be reunited someday in Heaven. How does this fact affect the way you view time and effort spent on relationships?

6. How does an eternal perspective affect the way you view your friends and family members who have never trusted in Jesus Christ for salvation?

AN ETERNAL PERSPECTIVE
CHANGES THE WAY WE VIEW DEATH

"But now that he is dead, why should I fast? Can I bring him back again? I will go to him, but he will not return to me." (2 Samuel 12:23)

7. After considering what David said in the verse above, think about a time when someone close to you died.

> a. At that time did you have an eternal perspective? If so, how did it help you? It not, how could it have helped you?

> b. Do you think that time heals the pain from the loss of a loved one? Why, or why not?

8. Have you ever really thought about your own death? Are you ready to die? Explain.

AN ETERNAL PERSPECTIVE
CHANGES THE WAY WE VIEW AGING

"This is the reason we never lose heart. The outward man does indeed suffer wear and tear, but every day the inward man receives fresh strength. These little troubles (which are really so transitory) are winning for us a permanent, glorious and solid reward out of all proportion to our pain." (2 Corinthians 4:16, PH)

9. How do you feel about getting older?

10. How does our culture view aging?

11. Think of someone you know who has aged gracefully and with an eternal perspective. Describe that person for the group. What impresses you most about him or her?

LOOKING TO GOD

Identify one area in your life where keeping an eternal perspective would bring rest to your life. (For example: grief after someone's death, your own aging or death, your business success or failure.) What steps can you take to cultivate an eternal perspective in that area? Select an idea from "Into Our Lives," or make up your own plan.

INTO OUR LIVES

1. Commit yourself to spending at least fifteen minutes a day this week reading your Bible. (Try reading through Genesis, then tackle Matthew. Either book should help with an eternal perspective.) Make this a priority over leisure activities such as television.

As you read, try to remember what you've learned in the past two sessions about forgiveness and limits. Watch for what Genesis and Matthew have to say about those two topics. How can an eternal perspective help you maintain a forgiving attitude and stay within God's limits?

2. Begin to cultivate a friendship with someone who is mature in his (or her) walk with the Lord. Ask that person to share a meal with you this week, or just spend an hour talking. Ask him how he maintains an eternal perspective on life, and how that perspective affects his life.

3. Memorize 1 Corinthians 2:9. Recite it to yourself daily this week, and think about how this truth can give you hope in the midst of your circumstances each day.

4. Tell a nonChristian friend that you are studying rest with a group of friends. In terms you think he (or she) can handle, describe a little of what you've learned about forgiveness, limits, or an eternal perspective. Avoid religious language, and be sensitive to what interests that person. Don't say too much.

Then ask your friend how hurried he feels his life is. Spend some time listening sensitively. Resist the temptation to overwhelm your friend with the whole gospel message; leave the door open for him to ask more if he's interested.

FOR MEDITATION

We take excellent care of our bodies, which we have for only a lifetime; yet we let our souls shrivel, which we will have for eternity.

Billy Graham

Let temporal things serve your use, but the eternal be the object of your desire.

Thomas á Kempis

He who provides for this life, but takes no care for eternity, is wise for a moment but a fool forever.

John Tillotson

He who has God and everything has no more than he who has God alone.

C. S. Lewis

You may get to the very top of the ladder, and then find it has not been leaning against the right wall.

A. Raine

We should not seek to escape from the temporal into the spiritual but rather to bring the spiritual to bear on the temporal.

Donald Bloesch
The Crisis of Piety

Rest in the Midst
of Suffering

WARM-UP

• What steps did you take this week to gain a more eternal perspective? Did you find your perspective better at times? Describe what happened.

• Think of a time in the past when you were suffering either emotionally or physically. What was your attitude at the time? What did that suffering do to your sense of inner rest?

THE FOURTH NECESSITY FOR REST: WE MUST LEARN TO ACCEPT OUR SUFFERING AND MAINTAIN A SERVANT ATTITUDE REGARDLESS OF OUR CIRCUMSTANCES

❝ I've made two observations about people who suffer. First, of all the obstacles to genuine rest, there is nothing that can drain it away faster than suffering. Second, suffering people who are willing to bring rest to their lives enjoy *a richer and better degree of rest* than those who rest without suffering.

When a person finds himself having to endure some discomfort or severe suffering, it's easy for him to go to one of two extremes. He either denies that it could actually be happening to him, or he assumes that God is going to intervene in some supernatural way and make the pain go away.

God *is* a God of miracles. He performs them all the time. But there is a difference between a God of miracles and a God of magic. Miracles are done for His glory, magic is performed for our entertainment. The normal human response to suffering is a plea to take it away. But God isn't required to do it, nor is it His standard way of handling our problems. Let's look at the life of Jesus to see how He responded to suffering.

Jesus knew that He was heading for a cross from the time He was born. During His three-year public ministry, He alluded several times to His ultimate destiny. But as He got closer to the cross, the human nature that hurts and feels rejection surfaced. At one point He fell on His face pleading with His Father to see if there was any way that "this cup could pass" from Him. He loved lost people and was committed to obeying His Father, but like any person with human feelings, He wanted to avoid the excruciating suffering that was awaiting Him on the cross.

An interesting thing happened once He accepted the inevitable. He got up off of the ground, wiped the tears and dirt from His face, and went to face His fate. Throughout the entire trial, flogging, ridicule, and crucifixion, Christ displayed a quiet, determined calm. It was wrapped up in His acceptance of the circumstances and His confidence in the divine plan between Himself and His Father.

I find it hard to understand, but at the one time in Jesus' earthly ministry when He needed to be concentrating on His own problems, He chose to accommodate the needs of others. In His example we find a key necessity for a rested heart. Jesus knew that rest doesn't come in serving self, but in serving others. He knew that His own pain could never be an excuse for ignoring the pain of others.

He looked down from the cross and saw the middle-aged woman who had, as a teenager, submitted to the God she loved and offered her womb as an incubator for the King of kings. Mary was graying now. With all that had transpired in the past few days, she looked beaten. He spoke to the one disciple He was sure would be responsible enough to fulfill His request. He asked John to make sure that she was cared for.

Jesus hung between social scum. He was the lily floating in the cesspool. But He knew He was dying to give hope to the very men with whom He was crucified. One thief mocked Him. The other asked Him for help. Jesus turned His tired and bloody head far enough to catch the man's eyes. He gave him a promise and a confidence that they would both be in paradise together. That man became the first convert of the crucified Lord. (The last shall be first.)

While people watched, men laughed, and soldiers gambled, Jesus turned His heart toward Heaven and prayed a prayer on their behalf. He said, "Father, forgive them. They haven't a clue of what they've done" (Luke 23:34, paraphrased).

Jesus found rest in accepting the cross and serving others. His example is vital to the suffering heart looking for rest. He said, "If anyone would come after me, he must deny himself and take up his cross and follow me" (Mark 8:34). He knew that we can't necessarily change the behavior of others, but we can control our attitudes. He said, "Love your enemies and pray for those who persecute you" (Matthew 5:44).

All this may sound like lame advice if you are in the middle of a suffering situation. What we *want* is relief. We want our problem or heartache to just go away. Yet the biblical message of rest is that your relief may come from the strength you develop from serving in spite of your suffering. You'll find a quiet calm awaiting you when you accept what you cannot change, and serve the very people who contribute to your pain.

(Adapted from chapter 7 of Little House on the Freeway.*)*

ACCEPTING AND SERVING

1. "Suffering people who are willing to bring rest to their lives enjoy *a richer and better degree of rest* than those who rest without suffering." What do you think of this statement?

2. Is there anything in Jesus' example that moves you to accept your suffering and serve in the midst of it? If so, what?

"When all kinds of trials and temptations crowd into your lives, my brothers, don't resent them as intruders, but welcome them as friends! Realize that they come to test your faith and to produce in you the quality of endurance. But let the process go on until that endurance is fully developed, and you will find you have become men of mature character, men of integrity with no weak spots." (James 1:2-4, PH)

3. What reasons does James give in the passage above for accepting our trials with joy?

4. Have you ever been in a situation where you were able to accept your trials as friends? If so, what enabled you to have this attitude?

5. Think about the most difficult thing you are experiencing in your life at this time. What factors make it especially difficult for you to accept this particular trial?

6. Does accepting your situation mean you don't have faith in God's ability to change things? Why, or why not?

7. Discuss the following statements. Which ones reflect a godly attitude of acceptance toward suffering?

- I accept my present circumstances and will do nothing to change them.
- I trust God even when He seems far away.
- I seek deeper understanding of God, and although I ask "why," I accept that my questions may never be answered.
- I wait expectantly for complete deliverance from my suffering in the here and now.
- I seek God and leave my future in His hands.
- I ask God for an explanation of my suffering and expect an answer.
- I seek a specific future that I believe will bring glory to God.
- I try not to pay attention to my feelings. Instead, I act as I think I'm supposed to.
- I express to God my darkest feelings, asking Him to forgive any resentment and anger.
- I ask God to give me the strength to carry on if He chooses not to remove my suffering.
- I resign myself to my situation and seek no help from other people.

"The thief comes only to steal and kill and destroy; I have come that they may have life, and have it to the full. . . .

"I have told you these things, so that in me you may have peace. In this world you will have trouble. But take heart! I have overcome the world." (John 10:10, 16:33)

8. a. It is often hard to accept suffering because we tend to expect life to be different. We feel we deserve certain things from God. According to Jesus' words in John 10:10 and 16:33, what can we rightfully expect from life?

b. How do you reconcile those statements from Jesus? What do you think He means?

▶c. If following Jesus guarantees that your life will be full of trouble, why bother?

"But the fruit of the Spirit is love, joy, peace, patience, kindness, goodness, faithfulness, gentleness and self-control. . . . Since we live by the Spirit, let us keep in step with the Spirit. Let us not become conceited, provoking and envying each other." (Galatians 5:22-26)

"Those who suffer according to God's will can safely commit their souls to their faithful Creator, and go on doing all the good they can." (1 Peter 4:19, PH)

9. First Peter 4:19 expresses both responses to suffering: trusting acceptance and service to others. According to Galatians 5:22-26, what attitudes do we need to have in order to concentrate on serving rather than on escaping or resenting pain?

LOOKING TO GOD
Allow a few minutes for individual silent prayer. Ask the Lord Jesus to enable you to follow His example in accepting the cross. Ask Him to help you accept your present trials with His attitude rather than with defeat, resentment, or rebellion. Ask Him how you can serve others in the midst of your suffering.

You may choose to share your feelings about your

circumstances. Be willing to explore how the Scripture says we should deal with those feelings in order to get past them to faith.

INTO OUR LIVES
During the week, complete the following personal inventory. Grade yourself on a scale of 1 (not at all) to 10 (completely).

___ I am prepared to accept the suffering God chooses to allow in my life.
___ I am accepting the trials I am presently facing.
___ I am cultivating Christlike qualities in my life:
   __ patience   __ a lack of self-centeredness
   __ faithfulness   __ a peaceful spirit
   __ self-control   __ self-control
   __ humility   __ a lack of envy
___ I am serving as God has enabled me in the midst of my present suffering.

Now spend some time talking to the Lord about changes you need to make. If you feel you have fallen short in all areas, confess your failures to God, tell Him how you feel, and ask Him to help you believe He forgives you.

Then focus on one specific area in which you would like to grow. Write it down, or put a star by it if it's on the list above. Finally, commit yourself to making this chosen area a part of your prayers this week. (For example: "My impatience often causes me to miss the lessons God is trying to teach me through trials. I'm so focused on getting past the trial that I miss any opportunity to grow. This week I will watch for times when I am impatient, and I will ask God to replace impatience with a quiet, teachable spirit.")

FOR MEDITATION
Our real blessings often appear to us in the shape of pains, losses and disappointments; but let us have patience, and we soon shall see them in their proper figures.

Joseph Addison

The stars are constantly shining, but often we do not see them until the dark hours.

Earl Riney

Affliction can be a treasure. Absolutely functional, it triggers life's greatest insights and accomplishments.

Fred Greve

Jesus did not come to explain away suffering or remove it. He came to fill it with His presence.

Paul Claudel

As believers we cannot always know why, but we can always know why we trust God who knows why, and this makes all the difference.

Os Guinness
In Two Minds

The ancient silver smith would heat crude silver ore in his crucible until the impurities rose to the top. Then he would skim off the slag and repeat the refining process. He knew he had achieved pure silver when, gazing into the molten metal, he could see his own reflection. Our Father disciplines us in the crucible of trial and suffering, then skims away the impurities. His goal is to look into our lives and see the image of Jesus (Romans 8:29).

Jim Carpenter, "Do You Know Your Father?"
Discipleship Journal, Volume 51

As sure as ever God puts His children in the furnace He will be in the furnace with them.

Charles H. Spurgeon

Learning Contentment

WARM-UP

- How did you do at serving in the midst of your suffering this week? What helped? What were the obstacles?
- Complete the following sentences privately, reflecting your present perspective on your life. List as many completions as you can in two minutes.

> a. If only I had . . . (For example: a better job, a specific lifestyle, taken more time with my family.)
> b. If only I hadn't . . . (For example: run up so many debts, started drinking, neglected my friends.)
> c. If only they had . . . (For example: recognized my potential, been honest with me, stuck with me.)
> d. If only they hadn't . . . (For example: discouraged me, lied to me, been ashamed of me.)

THE FIFTH NECESSITY FOR REST: WE MUST LEARN TO BE CONTENT THROUGH GODLY DESIRES AND EXPECTATIONS

❝ I remember one sad day when my grandmother was washing clothes. She was using an old-style wringer washing machine when she got her fingers too close to the wringers. Before she knew what had happened the two hungry rollers had pulled her arm in up to the elbow. In the shock and pain of the moment she couldn't think to hit the panic bar. Instead, she reversed the gears and rolled her mangled arm out the way that it had come in.

The consumption oriented society that you and I live

in takes us through a wringer of a different sort. It does this in a subtle but deliberate way: It simply keeps us *unsatisfied*. Our own artificially-created expectations wring rest from our hearts. They squeeze out our joy and leave our spirits dry and brittle.

No matter what we have, it isn't enough.

In order to have any hope of enjoying the rest God intends for me, I have to remind myself that I am in a constant struggle with my culture to maintain a sense of contentment. Keeping the average family discontent is vital to our economic system. In order to lure me to a particular product, an advertiser must create a dissatisfaction for what I have—or a nagging desire for things that I don't need.

In order to be content we must learn to discipline or control our desires. When people fail to discipline their desires, they feel incomplete. A gloomy cloud of inadequacy follows them around. It's difficult to maintain deep relationships with such people—their feelings of inadequacy drain your emotions. When people fail to control their desires, they give into the powers in the world system that desire to control them. A heart that finds it hard to accept its position in life is putty in the hands of the powers of darkness.

God used the first and last of the Ten Commandments as the supports for the other eight. They were sweeping statements that served as catchalls for the wandering passions of man. If we view these as guidelines for contentment (which they are), we will see why it makes such logical sense to place them in the order in which they appear in the Bible.

The first commandment says, "I am the LORD your God, who brought you out of Egypt, out of the land of slavery. You shall have no other gods before me" (Exodus 20:2-3).

A focused affection on the God who sets men free is the best way to enjoy a life of balanced love. God *is* love. He is the essence of its definition. Since love is one of the fundamental needs of man, it stands to reason that we need to begin by loving the Author of love.

62

The last commandment says, "You shall not covet your neighbor's house. You shall not covet your neighbor's wife, or his manservant or his maidservant, his ox or donkey, or anything that belongs to your neighbor" (Exodus 20:17).

Coveting has a lot of nasty synonyms: envy, jealousy, lust, greed. . . . It starts in our hearts as a seed but gets watered and fertilized by the inevitable pressures on our pride. Coveting is material inebriation. It's an addiction to things that don't last and a craving for things that don't really matter. It forces us to depend on tomorrow to bring us the happiness that today couldn't supply.

As we seek to have disciplined desires we must remember that there is a healthy desire within most of us to improve ourselves and our positions. It is an instinctive quality placed within us by God. To deny it would be foolish, and to ignore it would be sacrilegious.

But as we dream we must be sure to do two things. First, *we need to make sure that we are pursuing legitimate goals.* A legitimate goal is anything that improves your ability to love and serve God and people. Second, *we must make sure that we are making the most of where we are.* You know what I mean. You've seen people who are so busy stretching for the brass ring that they forget to enjoy the merry-go-ride.

We need to make contentment a member of our internal board of directors. Give him the freedom to ask the hard questions when you start feeling you need something more to bring you happiness. If you do, be prepared to mumble a lot to yourself. He likes to ask questions like these: Can you afford this? Do you have to give up much of the few spare hours that you have left to take advantage of this thing? Will this free you up to spend the time necessary to maintain your commitments to family and friends? Will this in any way frustrate your relationship with God?

Having godly expectations is another key to learning contentment. We must stop approaching life as if it owed us something. We are all given the opportunity to love and to hope. People with godly expectations and con-

63

tentment live life for what they have, not for what they could get. They don't demand anything from life. Life has a hard time letting them down. These people are serious and disciplined stewards of their expectations. They do not covet what they do not possess.

The only way we can develop godly expectations and desires is with God's help. A relationship with God that is personal yields a set of desires that are pleasing to God. Knowing that He loves us and has forgiven us keeps us from wanting the wrong things. By following His example when He walked the earth, we learn true contentment. *(Adapted from chapter 8 of* Little House on the Freeway.*)*

DISCIPLINING OUR DESIRES
1. What are some of the things that our culture says are requirements for contentment? Do you struggle with these standards? If so, how?

2. a. "A focused affection on the God who sets men free is the best way to enjoy a life of balanced love." How would you restate that in your own words?

   b. What has God done that motivates you to make Him your number one desire? How would God complete this sentence?

   "I am the Lord your God, who _____ .
   You shall have no other gods before Me."

3. a. What is the difference between having legitimate goals and coveting?

b. Do you find this contrast helpful? Why or why not?

"Delight yourself in the LORD and he will give you the desires of your heart." (Psalm 37:4)

4. a. According to Psalm 37:4, what condition must be met for our desires, dreams, and goals to be pleasing to God?

b. Do you think meeting this condition changes what we desire? If so, how?

5. Look back at the ways you completed the first sentence in the warm-up section.

a. Which of your desires seem to fit a life that is pleasing to God?

b. Which of your desires are not pleasing to God and may stand in the way of God's best for you?

6. Consider the regrets that you listed in the warm-up. Then give an example of how a past hurt can cause someone to desire the wrong things.

It is normal, yet foolish, to let past disappointments cause us to chase unhealthy desires. We need to be disciplined in keeping our past hurts in perspective. God wants to comfort our sorrows, fill our voids, and forgive our sins. (Remember your discussion in session 3.)

7. How would you feel if you were told that your present level of existence is the level that you will stay at for the rest of your life (income, housing, transportation, amenities, etc.)?

GODLY EXPECTATIONS
8. What is the bare minimum you expect God to provide for you?

▶**9.** Here is a list of some of the earthly blessings we often expect from God. Unless your time is limited, read each passage to see how God sometimes responds to these expectations.

- protection from death (Acts 7:54-60)
- protection from trouble (2 Corinthians 6:3-4)
- plenty to eat (2 Corinthians 6:5)
- others to understand us (2 Corinthians 6:6-9)
- a decent standard of living (2 Corinthians 6:10)
- good health (Philippians 2:25-30)

"Do not be anxious about anything, but in everything, by prayer and petition, with thanksgiving, present your requests to God. And the peace of God, which transcends all understanding, will guard your hearts and your minds in Christ Jesus." (Philippians 4:6-7)

10. In the last session we saw that Jesus Christ tells us to expect peace in the midst of trouble as we devote ourselves to God's agenda (John 16:33). In Philippians, the Apostle Paul agrees that if we turn our anxieties over to

God, He will give us His peace.
How does peace transform our expectations?

"I have learned to be content whatever the circumstances.
I know what it is to be in need, and I know what it is to
have plenty. I have learned the secret of being content
in any and every situation, whether well fed or hungry,
whether living in plenty or in want. I can do everything
through him who gives me strength." (Philippians 4:11-13)

12. According to Philippians 4:11-13, how does Paul cope
with unpredictable and often frustrating circumstances?

LOOKING TO GOD
Spend a couple of minutes in prayer—silently or aloud—
asking God to help you seek Him above all else and know
what it means to delight in Him. Ask Him for the strength
to let go of your ungodly desires and to replace them with
desires consistent with His purposes for your life. Tell
Him about your anxieties and how you feel about your
circumstances. Pray to receive peace and contentment.

INTO OUR LIVES
Choose one of the following personal responses to what
you've been discussing. Take time during the week to
think and pray through it.

1. a. Are you content or discontent with each of the following areas of your life?

- friendships
- family relationships
- church commitments
- living situation
- place of residence

- job
- car
- wardrobe
- health

b. Do you think your discontentment in any of these areas indicates that the Lord Jesus wants you to change the situation? If so, mark a "C" next to that item.

c. On the other hand, does your discontentment come from wrong desires or expectations? If so, mark a "W" next to that item.

d. Take a few minutes to confess your undisciplined desires and ungodly expectations to the Lord. Ask Him to help you see which expectations and desires you need to let go of. Ask Him to help you desire a close fellowship with Him above all else. Also, ask Him to show you how to change the situations that you can and should change.

2. Spend some time evaluating your present level of consumerism. On the following items, grade yourself on a scale of 1 (always) through 10 (never).

How often do I buy something . . .
___ I don't need?
___ because someone else has it?
___ because I'm feeling sorry for myself?
___ with money I don't really have?
___ I don't really need when bills remain unpaid?
___ on an impulse and later regret it?

Ask the Lord to help you become a more careful consumer. Make a commitment before Him to change your buying habits in an appropriate way. What immediate steps can you take?

3. Memorize Philippians 4:6-7 or 4:11-13. Use the passage to help you when the world tries to lure you into discontentment.

4. Keep track this week of when you feel discontented. Try to determine the cause. Seek ways to overcome the influences that try to rob you of contentment. Ask the Lord to help you sort out what you can change and what you need to accept.

FOR MEDITATION

Contentment consists not in adding more fuel, but in taking away some fire; not in multiplying of wealth, but in subtracting men's desires.

Thomas Fuller

The world is poor because her fortune is buried in the sky and all her treasure maps are of the earth.

Calvin Miller

The greatest wealth is contentment with little.

James Howell

The roots of our hearts have grown down into things, and we dare not pull up one rootlet lest we die. Things have become necessary to us, a development never originally intended. God's gifts now take the place of God, and the whole course of nature is upset by the monstrous substitution.

A. W. Tozer
The Pursuit of God

God, give us grace to accept with serenity the things that cannot be changed, courage to change the things which should be changed, and the wisdom to distinguish the one from the other.

Reinhold Niebuhr

Managing Our Strengths

WARM-UP

• What did you observe this week about your desires and expectations?
• Privately, list your three greatest weaknesses, as you see them. Then list your three greatest strengths. Now, as a group discuss: Was it harder for you to think of your strengths or your weaknesses? Why do you think this was the case?

THE SIXTH NECESSITY FOR REST:
WE MUST MANAGE OUR RESOURCES AND STRENGTHS

❝ Knowledge of our personal strengths is critical to a calm and ordered life. For most of us it is easy enough to list weaknesses. All of us have had plenty of help on that score. Parents, teachers, coaches, friends, and enemies made sure we didn't overlook a single one.

I have observed that most people grow up with a lot of negative reinforcement. Our culture occasionally rewards but seldom remembers those who come in second. The list of those who "also ran" doesn't get much space in the yearbook.

But the fact remains that you and I *do* have strengths: God-given resources worth developing and managing. If we want to cope with the incredible pressures of our hurried world, we need to isolate those strengths and put them to work. It's a matter of stewardship.

The word *stewardship* isn't used as much as it used to

be. But it's an excellent word. It refers to the *conscientious management of the things that really matter.* It requires responsibility and maturity. Stewardship demands work and doesn't accept excuses. It forces people to reevaluate priorities. It makes them reconsider their purposes for living.

When I meet older people advising me to slow down, spend more time with people, and develop my talents, I hear wise experience talking. Often, they have learned through waste and regret what God would rather teach us through principles of stewardship. They have learned that resources are to be conserved and invested, not ignored or squandered.

It will help us, as we develop this discussion on managing our gifts, to divide our true assets into three categories: *convictions, capabilities,* and *callings.* These groupings can serve as a checklist as we determine what kind of a steward we are.

Your convictions represent an incredible source of strength. Maybe you've never included them in an inventory of your personal resources before. Yet your personal convictions must be counted among your most precious possessions. The pressures to conform, to ignore, to excuse, or to surrender bombard us every day. If I want to maintain a calm heart in the midst of a hectic fast-paced culture, I must be careful to keep my convictions uncompromised.

That's why a steady diet of Bible reading and Bible study is so crucial to the well-managed life. The Bible's pages contain universal truths we can rely on when we aren't sure of what to do. In my work, I encounter all kinds of people. Those who make it through life with the least amount of conflicts from their personal choices are those who submit to a clear set of convictions. And those who submit to convictions invariably maintain a consistent intake of God's Word. I'm not legalistic about when or how often a person must read the Scriptures. I just know that those who come to the Bible on a habitual basis to gain direction for living make better choices.

The second resource we need to manage well is our

capabilities. Every person has talent. When talents are harnessed and disciplined they become skills. Many people run into problems because stewarding capabilities is hard. It means denying oneself, sacrificing, and failing in order to perfect what we are gifted at doing.

In addition to natural talents, every Christian has spiritual gifts. These were given by God in order to round out the church. Attending church Sunday after Sunday without serving is poor stewardship of our capabilities. God can bring us a depth of joy and stability when we are carefully guarding and using the talents and gifts He gave us.

Finally, we must be good stewards of our callings. Part of the frustration of the hurried life is that it has a way of trivializing our commitments. We have certain callings in life that must be maintained, but life hassles us into giving these callings a second-class status. Our callings can be divided into two categories: vocational and relational.

We may not all have a specific vocational calling, but we are all called into relationships where we must make commitments that require self-sacrifice and service. These relational callings are no less important to God than a specific vocational calling such as a teacher, doctor, or pastor. At times our vocational commitment can even come into conflict with our relational callings.

Being an effective parent and being a "success" at the same time is sometimes impossible. When it comes to choices in this area, the lure of the fast lane increases its pull. Kids don't reward our egos as much as the shiny steps at the top of the ladder of success. That's why the sixth key to rest carries so much clout. It's the acid test of our priorities. If we are good stewards of our callings we will consistently refuse to sacrifice the permanent on the altar of the immediate. We will place our callings in divine order. Regardless of how noble our vocation and how many people directly benefit from our involvement in it, God would not condone the forsaking of primary callings (marriage and children) for secondary callings (work).

(Adapted from chapter 9 of Little House on the Freeway.*)*

STEWARDING OUR CONVICTIONS

"Blessed is the man who does not walk in the counsel of the wicked or stand in the way of sinners or sit in the seat of mockers. But his delight is in the law of the LORD, and on his law he meditates day and night. He is like a tree planted by streams of water, which yields its fruit in season and whose leaf does not wither. Whatever he does prospers." (Psalm 1:1-3)

1. How does Psalm 1:1-3 describe the person who guards his convictions and keeps them in line with God's law?

2. What convictions of yours are often challenged by your friends, family, or acquaintances?

3. Think about how you can "steward" your convictions.

a. What can you do to keep your convictions consistent with the Lord's?

b. How can you guard against caving in when people urge you to violate your convictions?

STEWARDING OUR CAPABILITIES

"For by the grace given me I say to every one of you: Do not think of yourself more highly than you ought, but rather think of yourself with sober judgment, in accordance with the measure of faith God has given you. Just as each of us has one body with many members, and these members do not all have the same function, so in Christ we who are many form one body, and each member belongs to all the others. We have different gifts, according to the grace given us. If a man's gift is prophesying, let him use it in proportion to his faith. If it is serving, let him serve; if it is teaching, let him teach; if it is encouraging, let him encourage; if it is contributing to the needs of others, let him give generously; if it is leadership, let him govern diligently; if it is showing mercy, let him do it cheerfully." (Romans 12:3-8)

6. In Romans 12:3-8, the Apostle Paul puts our gifts into perspective.

a. How does he say we should view ourselves?

b. How does this perspective eliminate pride?

7. What do you perceive to be your . . .

gifts?

talents?

Poorly managed talents and gifts can become overtaxed. Many people's weaknesses are nothing more than strengths pushed to the limit. If we push our spiritual gifts to an extreme, we burn out. If we push our emotional gifts to an extreme, we get depressed. If we push our physical gifts to an extreme, we get sick.

8. In what areas of your life do you feel overtaxed? Are any of your strengths in danger of becoming weaknesses because you are abusing them?

STEWARDING OUR CALLINGS

"We constantly pray for you, that our God may count you worthy of his calling, and that by his power he may fulfill every good purpose of yours and every act prompted by your faith." (2 Thessalonians 1:11)

9. In what specific ways has God called you to use your gifts and talents? If you are dissatisfied with the way you are presently using your capabilities, what commitments might God be leading you to make?

10. Into what relationships has God called you to invest your time and talents at this point in your life?

11. Time is the one gift in our life that was given to us in a fixed amount. Each time we use it, it is forever spent. Does the way you spend your time adequately reflect the callings you listed in the last two questions? If not, what changes can you make?

INTO OUR LIVES

1. If you are unclear about your spiritual gifts, read the following excerpt from *A Compact Guide to the Christian Life*. Answer the questions and try to determine your gift(s).

How Can I Discover My Gift(s)?

"*Commitment.* Are you committed to *do* whatever God wants you to do, or are you just interested in understanding yourself? God won't reveal His gifts to you until you are committed to His agenda.

"*Experience.* What has and hasn't God given you to do? In what service has God blessed your efforts, and in what areas has He not? What opportunities for service have and haven't been open to you? Through past experience God shows us the areas where we can serve Him best.

"*Natural abilities and temperament.* Spiritual gifts aren't the same as natural abilities, but they often build on or are consistent with natural inclinations. A teacher may be a naturally good student supernaturally gifted to pass on what he learns.

"On the other hand, God may call and gift you for a function that leaves dormant some of your favorite natural abilities and challenges your temperament. He might call a shy musician or scientist to a public ministry alongside or even instead of his other work.

"*Other Christians' confirmation.* God can use other Christians to give us guidance in discovering our spiritual gifts. In what areas do others say you have blessed them? What do mature Christians say when you ask them for counsel?"[1]

2. Ask yourself the following question: "In what areas of my life am I failing to be a good steward of what God has given me?" Ask the Lord to help you discern what specific changes He wants you to make. Make a commitment to follow through.

FOR MEDITATION
When You are our strength, it is strength indeed, but when our strength is our own it is only weakness.

Augustine of Hippo

If by doing some work which the undiscerning consider "not spiritual work" I can best help others, and I inwardly rebel, thinking it is the spiritual for which I crave, when in truth it is the interesting and exciting, then I know nothing of Calvary love.

Amy Carmichael, *If*

Do not despise your situation. In it you must act, suffer, and conquer. From every point on earth, we are equally near to heaven and the infinite.

Henri Frederic Amiel

Our vocation is to live in the Spirit—not to be more and more remarkable animals, but to be the sons and companions of God in eternity.

Anthony Bloom

NOTE
1. *A Compact Guide to the Christian Life*, compiled by K. C. Hinckley (Colorado Springs, Colo.: NavPress, 1989), pages 20-21.

Entering God's Rest

WARM-UP

• How hurried was your week on a scale of 1 to 10?

1	2	3	4	5	6	7	8	9	10
Snoozing in the sun								Pedal to the metal	

• What changes have you experienced since you began this study on surviving life in the fast lane? What hasn't changed that you wish had?

PUTTING IT ALL TOGETHER

▲▲ As we travel down the highway of life we often wonder if we are on the right road. It is easy to feel as if we've been swept into the fast lane, driving beyond the speed limit, our lives out of our control. In this study we've taken a look at six necessities for a life of rest. These necessities serve as highway signs reminding us that we are in the driver's seat. We can make good choices based on yielding to the Executive Engineer and His priorities rather than the world's. In the final session of this study we will further apply these principles to the following areas of our lives: marriage, children, friendships, and work.

1. *We must forgive.* Individuals desiring rest in their marriages must be prepared to forgive. Marriages can't handle the long-term pressure of bitterness. Husbands and wives hurt each other. Sometimes it's accidental, other times it's intended. There must be a willingness to

crumble up lists of hurts and throw them in the trash can at the foot of the cross.

I know some people can list hurts that seem beyond forgiveness. That's why forgiveness must come through God's power. It is the only way to have rest where bitterness once festered. It is a gift you can give to your spouse, but it is also a gift you give to yourself. It means that you are willing to do something about the anger in your heart. It's a way of disciplining your love and bringing rest to your spirit.

2. *We must live our lives within the boundaries of God's Word.* Having God's perspective on success is imperative if a person wants to enjoy rest at work. True success is measured by who you are, not what you do. It's knowing that your value comes from God and doesn't need achievement and rewards in order to be realized. Knowing that God loves you enough to save you, forgive you, and guarantee your eternal destiny gives you the significance to be a true success. It frees you to use work as a vehicle to facilitate your family rather than a force that holds your family hostage.

We need to be courageous enough to disagree with the world's view of success. We might take some criticism, and we might not advance as quickly, but we can maintain rest in the middle of a work arena intoxicated with getting ahead.

3. *We must live against the backdrop of eternity.* We will find rest when we keep our priorities in line with an eternal perspective. Keeping in mind that people are eternal has a way of changing the way you treat them. Friendships are an investment in eternity. Friends provide support when we are hurting. They also keep us accountable. They become the "caution" signs and the guardrails that keep us out of danger. Support and accountability are crucial needs for the person pressured by the demands of life. The best way to get good friends is to be a good friend.

4. *We must learn to accept our suffering and maintain a servant attitude regardless of our circumstances.* The marriage vows are clear: "For better or for worse." For some this

will mean serving a beloved spouse through a long illness. It did for my friend Sidney. After a long day at work he would come home, dismiss the day nurse, and retire to the bedroom where he cared for his invalid wife. A catheter bag had to be emptied and a bed pan offered. He would take a clean wash cloth and warm water to wash the face of his bride. He would tell her all the good things about his day. Then he'd look into her eyes and tell her what he told her every night before she went to sleep and every morning when she woke up: "I love you, honey. You're my life, my love, and my wife."

5. *We must learn to be content through godly desires and expectations.* What most of us do when we come to a relationship is develop a formula for success that assumes our partner will act, think, and respond in certain ways. That is why most of us become disappointed with our spouse. We are expecting that individual to fulfill our formula for happiness. But we marry a person with a mind of his or her own and a unique set of unrealistic expectations!

What I need to do is come to a relationship with expectations that only cover me. After all, I'm the only person over whom I have any control. Instead of making my wife's actions a requirement for my success, I want to make my actions a commitment to her success. In other words, if my contentment is contingent on her cooperation, I'm sure to lack contentment. If, however, my contentment is wrapped up in bringing to my marriage all that I can offer without requiring anything in return, I am more likely to enjoy peace in my marriage. I shift my spouse from being the accommodator of my needs to being the object of my love.

6. *We must manage our resources and strengths.* Our children are a precious responsibility from God; we are called to steward them well. One aspect of this is to be good stewards of their emotions. I wish there was a way to hook a sign on every kid's chest just above the heart that said: HANDLE WITH CARE, FRAGILE EMOTIONS ON BOARD. I can't believe how careless some parents can be with their children's emotions. They thoughtlessly pre-

sume that kids have sophisticated emotions capable of processing input at a mature adult level. They're wrong. A parent can crush a child's spirit with a glance or a few poorly-chosen words. The fact is that their young emotions are delicate, and we need to be careful how we handle them.

Parents can give rest to their children's emotions by displaying affection. Affection—meaningful touch and affirming words—forms a wall of protection around a child's confidence. It's hard to feel insignificant when a mother and father are generous with affection.
(Adapted from chapters 10 and 11 of Little House on the Freeway.)

REST FOR THE WEARY
1. The excerpt above applies the principles of rest to some concrete situations. Which of these applications strikes closest to home in your life?

2. Take a few minutes to look back over the notes you made during this study. What points meant the most to you personally?

3. We recognize that day to day rest (rest from the rat race) is a process—a series of choices based on timeless principles from God's Word. However, do you think it is possible to enter God's rest once and for all and, thereby, change the way you struggle with the issues raised in this guide? Why, or why not?

"The fruit of righteousness will be peace; the effect of righteousness will be quietness and confidence forever. My people will live in peaceful dwelling places, in secure homes, in undisturbed places of rest." (Isaiah 32:17-18)

4. Jesus is our righteousness. To the extent that we surrender to Him, we will experience the benefits of righteousness in our own lives here in the fast lane. What are the benefits of righteousness, according to Isaiah 32:17-18?

5. Take another look at the six necessities for rest as covered in the last six sessions. (We might equally call them six aspects of righteousness.)

   a. Give an example of how you have successfully applied one of the six.

   b. In which of the six necessities have you made the most significant progress during this series?

   c. Which one do you still need to work on the most? How might you go about that?

6. What has helped you the most during this series to find rest in the Lord?

LOOKING TO GOD
Write out a prayer expressing to the Lord the area where you need the most help in your search for rest in Him.

Share this need with your group. Then take a few minutes to pray for each other. (Can you also commit to pray for one another for the next month in these areas of need?)

INTO OUR LIVES

Becoming good at things that build inner confidence and calm takes practice—and a dash of creativity! The following list might provide some cloud-seeding for a brainstorm or two of your own. (For more ideas, see "101 Ways to Give Rest to Your Family," *Little House on the Freeway,* pages 219-223.)

Have fun with your spouse and family—and get ready for a good rest.

1. Go on a dialogue date with your spouse (no movie).
2. Give each family member a hug for twenty-one days in a row (that's how long some experts say it takes to develop a habit).
3. Pick an evening each week in which all televisions will remain unplugged.
4. Take an afternoon off from work; surprise your child by excusing him from school and taking him to a ball game.
5. Take a walk as a family.
6. Write each member of your family a letter sharing why you value them.
7. Go to bed early (one hour before your normal bedtime) every day for a week.
8. Encourage each child to submit to you his most perplexing question, and promise him that you'll discuss it and do your best to answer it.
9. Finish fixing something around the house.
10. Tell your kids how you and your spouse met.
11. Sit down and write your parents a letter thanking them for a specific thing they did for you. (Don't forget to send it!)
12. Praise your spouse and children—in their presence—to someone else.

Help for Leaders

This guide is designed to be used in a group of four to twelve people. Because God has designed Christians to function as a body, we learn and grow more when we interact with others than we would on our own. If you are on your own, recruit other people to join you in working through this study. If you have a group larger than twelve we suggest that you divide into groups of six or so. With more than twelve people, you begin to move into a large group dynamic, and not everyone can participate.

The following pages are designed to help a discussion leader guide the group in an edifying time centered on God's truth. You can appoint one person to lead each session, or you can rotate leadership.

PREPARATION
Your aim as a leader is to create an environment that is conducive to study. You want the group members to feel comfortable with one another and to find the setting congenial.

Personal preparation. As the group leader, your most important preparation for each session is prayer. You will want to make your prayers personal, of course, but here are general suggestions.

• Pray that group members will be able to attend the discussion consistently. Ask God to enable them to feel free to share thoughts and feelings honestly, and to contribute their unique gifts and insights.

- Pray for group members' private times with God. Ask God to be active in nurturing each person.
- Ask God to give each of you new understanding and practical applications from Scripture as you talk. Pray that God will meet each person's unique needs.
- Ask the Holy Spirit for guidance in exercising patience, acceptance, sensitivity, and wisdom. Pray for an atmosphere of genuine love in the group, with each member being honestly open to learning and change.
- Pray that your discussion will lead each of you to obey the Lord more closely and demonstrate His presence.
- Pray for insight as you go over the study materials and for wisdom as you lead the group.

After prayer, your most important preparation is to be thoroughly familiar with the material you will discuss. Before each meeting, be sure to answer all of the questions and read the leader's material for that session. You will also find it helpful to read the corresponding chapters in the book *Little House on the Freeway.*

Group preparation. Choose a time and place to meet that is consistent, comfortable, and relatively free from distractions. Refreshments can help people mingle, but don't let them consume your time.

THE FIRST SESSION

You may want to begin with a potluck supper. In this way, group members can get to know one another in the context of a meal, which is a good way to break down barriers. Then after dinner you can have your first session.

In this session, be sure to set aside adequate time for people to share who they are. It is amazing how much more productive and honest a Bible discussion is if the participants know each other.

At some point in the evening (probably toward the end), go over the following guidelines. They help make a discussion more fruitful, especially when you are dealing with issues that truly matter to people.

Confidentiality. No one should repeat what someone shares in the group unless that person gives permission. Even then, discretion is imperative. Be trustworthy. Participants should talk about their own feelings and experiences, not those of others.

Attendance. Each session builds on the previous ones, and you need continuity from each other. Ask group members to commit to attending all nine sessions, unless an emergency arises.

Participation. This is a *group* discussion, not a lecture. It is important that each person participate in the group.

Honesty. Appropriate openness is a key to a good group. Be who you really are, not who you think you ought to be.

LEADING THE GROUP
Each session is designed to take sixty minutes:

- Ten minutes for opening prayer and warm-up;
- Forty minutes for reading the text, discussing the questions, and choosing an application from the "Into Our Lives" section; and
- Ten minutes for closing prayer.

Work toward a relaxed and open atmosphere. This may not come quickly, so the leader must model acceptance, openness to truth and change, and love. Develop a genuine interest in each person's remarks, and expect to learn from them. Show that you care by listening carefully. Be affirming. Sometimes a hug is the best response.

Pay attention to how you ask the questions. Don't ask "What did you get for question 1?" Instead, by your tone of voice convey (1) your interest and enthusiasm for the question and (2) your warmth toward the group. The group will adopt your attitude. Read the questions as though you were asking them to good friends.

If the discussion falters:

- Be comfortable with silence. Let the group wrestle to think of answers. Don't be quick to jump in and

rescue the group with your answers.
- Reword a question if the group has trouble understanding it.
- If a question evokes little response, feel free to leave it and move on.
- You may want to answer questions yourself occasionally. In particular, you should be the first one to answer questions about personal experiences. In this way you will model the depth of openness and thought you hope others will show. You can also model an appropriate length of response. Don't answer every question, but don't be a silent observer.
- If the discussion is winding down on a question, go on to the next one. It's not necessary to push people to see every possible angle.

Ask only one question at a time. Often, participants' responses will suggest a follow-up question to you. Be discerning as to when you are following a fruitful train of thought and when you are going off on a tangent.

Be aware of time. Don't spend so much time discussing that you run out of time for prayer. Your goal is not to have something to discuss, but to become more like Jesus Christ.

Encourage constructive controversy. The group can learn a lot from struggling with the many sides of an issue. If you aren't threatened when someone disagrees, the whole group will be more open and vulnerable. Intervene, when necessary, making sure that people debate ideas and interpretations of Scripture, not attack each other's feelings or character. If the group gets stuck in an unresolvable argument, say something like, "We can agree to disagree here," and move on.

Don't be the expert. People will stop contributing if they think that you are judging their answers or that you think you know best. Let the Bible be the expert—the final say. Let people candidly express their feelings and experiences.

Don't do for the group what it can do for itself. With a beginning group, you may have to ask all of the questions, and do all of the planning. But within a few meetings you should start delegating various leadership responsibilities. Let members learn to exercise their gifts. Let them start making decisions and solving problems together. Encourage them to maturity and unity in Christ.

Encourage people to share feelings as well as facts. There are two dimensions of truth: the truth about how people feel, and the truth about who God is and what is right. People need to face their real feelings *and* the real God.

Summarize the discussion frequently. Summarizing what has been said will help the group see where the discussion is going.

Let the group plan applications. The group and individual action responses in the "Into Our Lives" section are suggestions. Your group should adapt them so that they are relevant and life-changing for the members. If group members aren't committed to an application, they won't do it. Encourage, but don't force.

End with refreshments. Have some coffee or soft drinks plus a snack, so that people will have an excuse to stay for a few extra minutes and discuss the subject informally. Often the most life-changing conversations occur after the formal session.

SUGGESTIONS FOR THE LEADER
Session 1
You or someone else in the group should open the session with a short prayer dedicating your time together to the Lord.

The purpose of this week's "Warm-up" is to get acquainted and establish a warm and open atmosphere for subsequent discussions. As you begin a new study, it is helpful to discover some of each others' experiences of the topic. Give each person one minute to answer the questions. You should go first, modeling openness and brevity (you might want to read one day's schedule from your calendar as an illustration of your complicated life). Try not to spend more than ten minutes on this warm-up, so that you will have plenty of time for the rest of your discussion.

Have a few people take turns reading aloud "The Hurried Home." Then move right into the "Personal Reflection" section. You will need to move the discussion from one question to the next before all possible discussion has been exhausted.

In chapter 1 of *Little House on the Freeway*, I sketch the various hurried families in much more detail. It is a good idea to read that chapter before your group meets. You might want to bring the book with you. Then, if someone in your group doesn't quite understand what I am getting at in the discussion guide, you can use the book to clarify. As a general rule, you will probably find it helpful to read the relevant chapter(s) of *Little House on the Freeway* before each group meeting even if the rest of your group isn't reading it.

In session 1, there are arrows (▶) beside questions 2 and 3. An arrow denotes an optional question. If your time is limited, you can omit one of these questions.

Be sure to save at least five minutes for group members to read through "Into Our Lives" and choose an action to take before your next meeting. The "Warm-up" in session 2 will include reporting on lessons learned from this activity.

Perhaps most important of all is to allow time to pray together at the end of the session. Any problems discussed during the session should be items for prayer. If your group is new to praying together, you could go around the circle a few times, letting each person offer a sentence of prayer. The first time around, let people confess to God one way in which their lives are hurried (they can't relax, can't enjoy quiet, etc.). The second time around, let each person ask God to bring rest to the person on his or her left. You can go first each time to model the prayer. If your group is more comfortable praying aloud, you can have open, conversational prayer for each other's needs. Close by thanking Jesus for offering you rest.

On your own, after the session, use the following evaluation questions to help improve your leadership next time:

• Did you have the right number of questions prepared? Should you add to the next session's questions, or delete some?

• Did you discuss the major issues?

• Did you know your material thoroughly enough to have freedom in leading?

• Did you keep the discussion from wandering?

• Did everyone participate? Were people open?

• Was anyone overly talkative? Overly quiet? Disruptive?

• Was the discussion practical? Did it lead to new understanding, hope, repentance, or change?

• Did you begin and end on time?

• Did you give the group the maximum responsibility that it can handle?

• What problems did these questions point out? Think about how you can handle these problems next week if they occur again.

Session 2

Select someone to open the meeting in prayer. Then ask two or three people to share what they learned from their application during the week (from "Into Our Lives").

Some group members will probably say they didn't have time to take any action steps because they were too busy. You will need to be sensitive to discern how to respond. Don't push people to perform for your approval; instead, look for ways to build them up.

Have five people read aloud a section of "Grace for Our Needs." The discussion revolves around how God meets our three inner needs. If you sense that one of the three is of prime importance to your group, feel free to concentrate your discussion on that one. It may be difficult to cover all three inner needs in one session.

Save ten minutes for prayer in triads. Encourage people who don't know each other well to join together. If your group doesn't divide perfectly in threes, one or two pairs will be fine.

If some group members are like the Moores described in session 1—people who constantly do things for others to earn approval—don't choose the third action step from "Into Our Lives." Discourage such people from selecting action number 2. On the other hand, if you tend to have a self-focused group, actions 2 and 3 might help them break out of their introspection.

Session 3

The second warm-up question has the potential to eat up a large chunk of your time. However, it is very helpful for members of the group to reinforce what they've learned by telling others. They can learn from each other and sort out frustrations and questions together. But you probably don't want to shortchange or postpone your discussion of the new material, unless you sense that your group will benefit from postponing session 3 for a week and you have the time. If you can't postpone session 3, cut off the warm-up discussion quickly, and encourage group members to gather informally after the meeting to finish this discussion.

There is a moving illustration of forgiveness in the fourth chapter of *Little House on the Freeway*, pages 56-61. If time permits, you may want to read this aloud during your group time.

Encourage everyone to spend time this week on one of the application exercises. Both choices involve memorizing a verse. This may be a new process for some group members. Tell the group that everyone will be encouraged to recite a verse next week. You might share the following benefits of Scripture memorization:

- *Disciplines* the mind to focus on the things of God.
- *Allows* for meditation on a verse.
- *Provides* accessibility to verses anytime, anywhere.
- *Replaces* anxiety and sinful thoughts with God's encouragement.
- *Protects* from sin.
- *Strengthens* in times of temptation and distress.

Begin your closing prayer time by allowing each person to say a short prayer thanking God the Father for the forgiveness we have because of Jesus Christ. Then pray for specific needs of group members.

Session 4

If you are meeting for only an hour, don't let the warm-up questions eat up more than ten minutes of your time.

Some people have trouble describing how they *feel* about something like rules (second warm-up question). They may not be aware that they are obsessed with rules, or that they detest them. So give people time and any necessary help in articulating how they feel. Don't put words into their mouths, but ask questions that rephrase what they are saying: "Do you mean that you like orderliness but you don't like being told what to do?"

The second warm-up question is designed to get people to think about how they react to rules in general. These attitudes may carry over to their response to God's "rules" or guidelines for living. People react to rules in different ways. Recognizing their initial responses to rules on a feeling level can help them understand patterns of rebellion toward God's commands and guidelines.

For instance, some people who have suffered from arbitrary and unfair rules develop patterns of resistance to rules in general. Recognizing such habit patterns may help them respond differently to God's guidelines, which bring true freedom and blessing. Other people are obsessed with rules in a legalistic way. Recognizing their legalism will free them to respond to God's limits out of love and understanding, instead of fear of disapproval.

You will not have time to discuss all the examples in question 5, but take time to read them all as a group. Then select those that are most relevant to your group.

This is a good time for you as the leader to reevaluate the progress of the group. Ask yourself the following questions:

> • Is the group interacting well? Are all members participating in the discussions? If one member is overly quiet, maybe you need to help draw this person out in a non-threatening way. Maybe a phone call would

be helpful. Ask the person how he or she is feeling about the study.

● Are friendships being formed in the group? What could be done to encourage this bond of friendship? Perhaps a potluck supper or a family game night with dessert would help give people a chance to get to know each other better.

● Are people applying the discussion to their lives? Are they participating in the "Into Our Lives" section?

● Are you praying for each person in your group during the week?

● Is there anyone in your group who needs extra encouragement? Perhaps a phone call from you this week would mean a lot.

Session 5

You probably won't have enough time to discuss how an eternal perspective affects how you view all four areas: people, love, death, and aging. Before your group meets, think about which two of these four you think your group most needs to think about. (Include either aging or death, since these are issues most modern people prefer to avoid.) Plan to discuss these two areas first, then the other two if time allows.

Be sure you save at least ten minutes for "Looking to God." Allow group members a couple of minutes to think of answers. Then let them share their answers with the group. Finally, take five minutes to pray for each other's needs, especially to gain an eternal perspective in the areas each person has mentioned.

To encourage group interaction, ask each person to call someone in the group this week to see how that person is keeping an eternal perspective amid the hassles of daily life. Designate whom each person is to call so that everyone gets one call and everyone makes one call.

Session 6

You may have trouble getting through all of the questions, especially if your group has passionate feelings about suffering. Be sure to cut the discussion off with at least five minutes to spare for the "Looking to God" section.

This can be a valuable chance for group members to air their feelings about their circumstances and receive compassion and encouragement. Provide an atmosphere in which it is safe for people to say how they really feel; but don't let complaining dominate your discussion. Acknowledge people's feelings and commend their honesty, but then move on to exploring how Scripture says we should deal with those feelings. If someone in your group seems to need more time to vent his feelings in order to get past them to faith, say something like, "Bob, I can see you are really hurting. After the meeting, let's set a time when we can talk this through. I don't want you to bury those thoughts just because our time here is limited." A hug might be appropriate.

Encourage everyone to take the time this week to do the personal inventory on page 59. This inventory is designed to help people identify areas where growth is needed in order to find rest in the midst of suffering.

Session 7
After everyone has completed the warm-up sentences, you may want to give each person a chance to share one sentence with the group. The purpose of this exercise is to help people become aware of the expectations from the past and present that may be robbing them of rest. Make sure that the discussion doesn't slip into an extensive analysis of one person's past.

In preparation for the session you will need to be aware of what Christian counseling services are available through your local church or in the community, in case someone needs additional help in dealing with unresolved disappointments from the past.

Session 8
In preparation for this session you will want to be clear on the difference between gifts and talents. There is helpful information on pages 76-77.

Before the session, think about the people in your group. What do you see as their gifts and talents? What gifts have been displayed during your group sessions? Has one person stood out as particularly helpful, always ready to serve? Has someone shown extra compassion, displaying the gift of mercy? What about the gift of teaching? Maybe there is a person in the group who has a way of making things clear for the others in the group. Your awareness of these things will be very helpful to the people in your group who may be unaware of their gift(s).

Session 9

There are additional applications of the six necessities for rest in the last four chapters of the book *Little House on the Freeway*. As the leader, you may find it helpful to be familiar with this material before your group meets for this final study session.

This study guide has skimmed the surface of the content within the book *Little House on the Freeway*. This may be the time to encourage the group members to read the entire book over the next few weeks. It would be a strong reinforcement to the principles you have been studying in your small group.

An extended prayer time would be appropriate for the end of this session. Encourage everyone to pray for the other members of the group during the next month.

You might consider having a final meeting one month from your last session. This could be a time of fellowship when people talk about the progress they have made in finding rest.